FORT WORTH LIBRARY

S0-BAG-163

CHILDREN 305.23 STRANGE
  2011
Strange, Matthew
Jump ropes, jacks, and
  endless chores
Summerglen   01/11/2011

SUMMERGLEN BRANCH

JUMP ROPES, JACKS, AND ENDLESS CHORES
Children's Lives in the 1800s

DAILY LIFE IN AMERICA IN THE 1800s

JUMP ROPES, JACKS, AND ENDLESS CHORES
Children's Lives in the 1800s

by
Matthew Strange

Mason Crest Publishers

Copyright © 2011 by Mason Crest Publishers. All rights reserved. No part of this publication may be reproduced or transmitted in any form or by any means, electronic or mechanical, including photocopying, recording, taping, or any information storage and retrieval system, without permission from the publisher.

MASON CREST PUBLISHERS INC.
370 Reed Road
Broomall, Pennsylvania 19008
(866)MCP-BOOK (toll free)
www.masoncrest.com

First Printing
9 8 7 6 5 4 3 2 1

Library of Congress Cataloging-in-Publication Data

Strange, Matthew.
  Jump ropes, jacks, and endless chores : children's lives in the 1800s / by Matthew Strange.
      p. cm. — (Daily life in America in the 1800s)
  ISBN 978-1-4222-1782-5 (hardcover)   ISBN (series) 978-1-4222-1774-0
  ISBN 978-1-4222-1855-6 (papercover)   ISBN (pbk series) 978-1-4222-1847-1
  1. Children—United States—History—19th century—Juvenile literature. 2. Childhood—United States—History—19th century—Juvenile literature. I. Title.
  HQ792.U5S77 2011
  305.230973'09034—dc22
                                  2010024703

Produced by Harding House Publishing Service, Inc.
www.hardinghousepages.com
Interior Design by MK Bassett-Harvey.
Cover design by Torque Advertising + Design.
Printed in USA by Bang Printing.

Contents

Introduction

History can too often seem a parade of distant figures whose lives have no connection to our own. It need not be this way, for if we explore the history of the games people play, the food they eat, the ways they transport themselves, how they worship and go to war—activities common to all generations—we close the gap between past and present. Since the 1960s, historians have learned vast amounts about daily life in earlier periods. This superb series brings us the fruits of that research, thereby making meaningful the lives of those who have gone before.

The authors' vivid, fascinating descriptions invite young readers to journey into a past that is simultaneously strange and familiar. The 1800s were different, but, because they experienced the beginnings of the same baffling modernity were are still dealing with today, they are also similar. This was the moment when millennia of agrarian existence gave way to a new urban, industrial era. Many of the things we take for granted, such as speed of transportation and communication, bewildered those who were the first to behold the steam train and the telegraph. Young readers will be interested to learn that growing up then was no less confusing and difficult then than it is now, that people were no more in agreement on matters of religion, marriage, and family then than they are now.

We are still working through the problems of modernity, such as environmental degradation, that people in the nineteenth century experienced for the first time. Because they met the challenges with admirable ingenuity, we can learn much from them. They left behind a treasure trove of alternative living arrangements, cultures, entertainments, technologies, even diets that are even more relevant today. Students cannot help but be intrigued, not just by the technological ingenuity of those times, but by the courage of people who forged new frontiers, experimented with ideas and social arrangements. They will be surprised by the degree to which young people were engaged in the great events of the time, and how women joined men in the great adventures of the day.

When history is viewed, as it is here, from the bottom up, it becomes clear just how much modern America owes to the genius of ordinary people, to the labor of slaves and immigrants, to women as well as men, to both young people and adults. Focused on home and family life, books in this series provide insight into how much of history is made within the intimate spaces of private life rather than in the remote precincts of public power. The 1800s were the era of the self-made man and women, but also of the self-made communities. The past offers us a plethora of heroes and heroines together with examples of extraordinary collective action from the Underground Railway to the creation of the American trade union movement. There is scarcely an immigrant or ethic organization in America today that does not trace its origins to the nineteenth century.

This series is exceptionally well illustrated. Students will be fascinated by the images of both rural and urban life; and they will be able to find people their own age in these marvelous depictions of play as well as work. History is best when it engages our imagination, draws us out of our own time into another era, allowing us to return to the present with new perspectives on ourselves. My first engagement with the history of daily life came in sixth grade when my teacher, Mrs. Polster, had us do special projects on the history of the nearby Erie Canal. For the first time, history became real to me. It has remained my passion and my compass ever since.

The value of this series is that it opens up a dialogue with a past that is by no means dead and gone but lives on in every dimension of our daily lives. When history texts focus exclusively on political events, they invariably produce a sense of distance. This series creates the opposite effect by encouraging students to see themselves in the flow of history. In revealing the degree to which people in the past made their own history, students are encouraged to imagine themselves as being history-makers in their own right. The realization that history is not something apart from ourselves, a parade that passes us by, but rather an ongoing pageant in which we are all participants, is both exhilarating and liberating, one that connects our present not just with the past but also to a future we are responsible for shaping.

—Dr. John Gillis, Rutgers University Professor of History Emeritus

1800   1801   1803   1804

1800 The Library of Congress is established.

1801 Thomas Jefferson is elected as the third President of the United States.

1803 Louisiana Purchase—The United States purchases land from France and begins westward exploration.

1804 Journey of Lewis and Clark— Lewis and Clark lead a team of explorers westward to the Columbia River in Oregon.

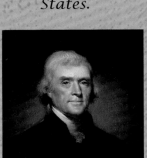

Time Line

1825   1832   1836   1837

1825 The Erie Canal is completed— This allows direct transportation between the Great Lakes and the Atlantic Ocean.

1832 New England unions condemn child labor— The New England Association of Farmers, Mechanics and Other Workingmen say child labor must have limits.

1836 Massachusetts becomes the first state to make a law restricting child labor by mandating that all workers under the age of 15 attend at least three months of school a year.

1837 Horace Mann becomes Secretary of Education in Massachusetts.

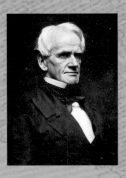

1812

1812 War of 1812—Fought between the United States and the United Kingdom.

1820

1820 Missouri Compromise—Agreement passed between pro-slavery and abolitionist groups, stating that all the Louisiana Purchase territory north of the southern boundary of Missouri (except for Missouri) will be free states, and the territory south of that line will be slave.

1821

1821 The first public high school in the United States opens in Boston.

1823

1823 Monroe Doctrine—States that any efforts made by Europe to colonize or interfere with land owned by the United States will be viewed as aggression and require military intervention.

1838

1838 Trail of Tears—General Winfield Scott and 7,000 troops force Cherokees to walk from Georgia to a reservation set up for them in Oklahoma (nearly 1,000 miles). Around 4,000 Native Americans die during the journey.

1839

1839 The first camera is patented by Louis Daguerre.

1844

1844 First public telegraph line in the world is opened—between Baltimore and Washington.

1848

1848 Seneca Falls Convention—Feminist convention held for women's suffrage and equal legal rights.

1848(-58) California Gold Rush—Over 300,000 people flock to California in search of gold.

1848 Pennsylvania passes law that sets minimum working age for children at 12.

1854

1854 Kansas-Nebraska Act—States that each new state entering the country will decide for themselves whether or not to allow slavery. This goes directly against the terms agreed upon in the Missouri Compromise of 1820.

1861

1861(-65) Civil War—Fought between the Union and Confederate states.

1862

1862 Emancipation Proclamation—Lincoln states that all slaves in Union states are to be freed.

1862 Homestead Act passed, promising 160 acres of free land to any U.S. citizen. To keep their land, settlers had to build homes and "improve" upon the land.

1865

1865 Thirteenth Amendment to the United States Constitution—Officially abolishes slavery across the country.

1865 President Abraham Lincoln is assassinated on April 15.

1876

1876 Alexander Graham Bell invents the telephone.

1876 Mark Twain's "Tom Sawyer" is first published.

1877

1877 Great Railroad Strike—Often considered the country's first nationwide labor strike.

1878

1878 Thomas Edison patents the phonograph on February 19.

1878 Thomas Edison invents the light bulb on October 22.

1886

1886: The Statue of Liberty is dedicated on October 28.

1867

1867 United States purchases Alaska from Russia.

1867 New Jersey becomes the first state in the Union to ban corporal punishment in schools.

1867 The Federal Department of Education is founded to assess the educational needs of American children in states across the country.

1869

1868 Louisa May Alcott's "Little Women" is published for the first time.

1869

1869 Transcontinental Railroad completed on May 10.

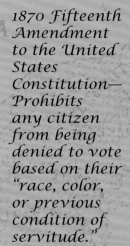

1870

1870 Fifteenth Amendment to the United States Constitution—Prohibits any citizen from being denied to vote based on their "race, color, or previous condition of servitude."

1870 Christmas is declared a national holiday.

1890

1890 Wounded Knee Massacre—Last battle in the American Indian Wars.

1892

1892 Ellis Island is opened to receive immigrants coming into New York.

1896

1896 Plessy vs. Ferguson—Supreme Court case that rules that racial segregation is legal as long as accommodations are kept equal.

1896 Henry Ford builds his first combustion-powered vehicle, which he names the Ford Quadricycle.

1898

1898 The Spanish-American War—The United States gains control of Cuba, Puerto Rico, and the Philippines.

Part I
Play

Can you imagine what life would be like if you didn't have to go to school every day? Sounds pretty good, right? What if you were trusted with an axe by age nine and a gun by age eleven? Kind of cool, huh?

Well, maybe.

Now imagine you were expected to work on a farm every day instead, wake up at the crack of dawn (or before) and help your dad plow the fields, or help your mom milk the cows. Think about what it would be like to have very few friends, to have to share your house with your extended family, and to have to look after all the children younger than you until the day you were old enough to do work on your own.

Not having to go to school all of a sudden doesn't seem so wonderful!

The lives of Americans in general during the 1800s were different from what they are today in many ways. But the experiences of children from the nineteenth century demonstrate some of the largest contrasts between now and then. Adults still worked back then, were expected to raise the kids, and took care of the house. Sure, the jobs might have been different—there were no computer programmers or pilots—but essentially, the movement of the adult day was similar to what it is today. Adults woke up, worked, took

Feeding the farm animals was a standard chore for many children in the 1800s.

care of the kids, went to sleep, and then woke up the next day and did it all over again. For children though, life was almost nothing like it is today, especially at the beginning of the nineteenth century. From 1800 until about the 1830s, children's lives were almost entirely focused inward, on the home.

Finding Time to Play

In the 1800s, some children went to school; most children worked, in one way or another; but as has always been the case, most children also found ways to play. Jumping rope had existed for a long time, but combined with the chanting of rhymes, it became a favorite pastime for American children in the middle of the nineteenth century. Young girls enjoyed playing with small wooden or cloth dolls, and boys could be seen shooting marbles. Pick-up-sticks, a game invented and played for centuries by American Indian children, was also played by children of the nineteenth century.

Other games were popular as well in the 1800s. There were no television sets, no computers, no video games, but there were always enough people around

While the boys were playing marbles in the school-yard, many of the girls were jumping rope. This is a picture of a fashionable girl (right)—but on the frontier, girls with far less elaborate wardrobes also enjoyed the fun and exercise of jumping rope. Farm children enjoyed playing in the hay (below).

Playing marbles was a favorite pastime of many children in the 1800s, especially boys.

for playing games. Families were large; parents and several children, as well as an aunt, uncle, or a grandparent or two, often lived under one roof. Wealthier folks who owned large houses would have a special room called a parlor, where people would gather in the evenings (much like the living room of today). A whole set of entertainments were called "parlor games," which both children and adults enjoyed. These included charades, Blind Man's Buff, guessing games, word games, and table games.

Dominoes was one of the favorite table games of the 1800s, and checkers (or "draughts") was another favorite. Tiddlywinks was a game where players used a disk called a shooter to flip smaller disks called winks into a cup that sat in the middle of the playing area. The object of the game was to be the first player to sink all of his or her disks into the cup. In the nineteenth century, players took this game very seriously and practiced flipping winks in their spare time.

Children also played card games and board games. In the nineteenth century, children's card games were designed to be educational. They helped children learn about arithmetic, history, and geography. Some card games even taught girls

Tiddlywinks was sometimes played with a set like this—but it could also be played on a kitchen table with a cup in the center.

The game of battledore was played much like the modern game of badminton.

cooking facts. Board games also had themes that were intended to improve children's minds. Some of these taught morality. For example, in Snakes and Ladders, the ladder squares had pictures of children doing good deeds, while the snake squares had pictures of children being disobedient.

Various forms of card games and table games were also popular in the 1800s. These children are playing Lotto.

But not all children's play was as quiet and decorous as what went on in the parlor. Most children in the 1800s also found time to play outdoors, and these games were noisier and more active. A favorite was Annie Over, a game that required two teams, a ball, and some kind of barrier, like a log or a table. Teams stood on either side of the barrier, and the team with the ball would yell, "Annie!" and throw the ball to a member of the opposing team. If the child on the other team catches the ball, the teams have to change sides—fast! While the teams are running to change sides, the one who caught the ball tries to hit an opponent with the

Hoops were popular toys for both boys and girls. These two children are boys, dressed in the most stylish Eastern fashions.

For farm children, the barn's hay mow made a wonderful place to play on rainy days.

ball. The goal is to eliminate the other team. Children also gathered in the streets or fields to play team games, including baseball and football (sometimes called rugby).

Both boys and girls played these games, but some games were not shared by the sexes. Graces, for example, was considered a "girls' game." It involved tossing a hoop back and forth between two players, using a stick, and it was meant to encourage girls to move gracefully.

Ring toss could be an inside or outdoor game.

EXTRA! EXTRA!

The Juvenile Gazette, 1828
Providence, Rhode Island
Oliver Kendall, Jr.

RUNNING

Is a very natural, healthful and innocent exercise for children. Some little boys have run races on foot for a wager, as horse racers do; this ought never to be done by old or young. All wagers are wrong.

MARBLES

Playing at marbles is a pretty amusement for boys; but they should never make it a game to win each other's marbles.

FLYING THE KITE

Flying the kite is an agreeable and innocent amusement for the good little boys in summer. Indeed it is pleasing to see to what a height they will soar, and the many curious motions they make, ascending, descending, &c. seeming to act as if alive. But still it is against the law, for horses are often frightened by them.

SKATING

This delightful diversion and exercise is superior to every thing that can be classed under the head of motion. Like the bird sailing through the air with wings unmoved, the skater glides along as if impelled by the mere energy of his will, gracefully wheeling in all the intri-

Children have been flying kites for centuries.

In nineteenth-century Boston, ice skating was a favorite pastime for both adults and children.

cate curves fancy can conceive, securely on the slippery surface that the unpracticed foot dares not tread, with a rapidity and ease that astonish us.

JUMPING THE ROPE

This is an excellent exercise for little boys and girls; indeed it is very pleasing to see with what nimbleness and delight they leap the cord. It is a play very suitable after confinement of 3 or 4 hours to a seat, to exercise the limbs & circulate the blood.

SLEDDING

Riding down hill is a dear bought pleasure. How often do we see the little fellows tugging up the steep hill through frost or snow, pulling their little sleds behind them, which they get upon and away they go; and in a very short time, if not overset by the way, they are at the bottom, and ready for another toil after a short pleasure.

Sledding was as popular an activity for children in the 1800s as it is today.

The life of little girls living in big Eastern cities was very different from the lives of frontier children. Catherine Haven (see next page) was cared for by a "nurse" (a nanny), and she was very interested in fashion!

EYEWITNESS ACCOUNT

Excerpts from Diary of a Little Girl in Old New York, by Catherine Elizabeth Havens

August 6, 1849.

I am ten years old today, and I am going to begin to keep a diary. My sister says it is a good plan and when I am old, and in a remembering mood, I can take out my diary and read about what I did when I was a little girl. . . .

We moved from Lafayette Place to Brooklyn when I was four years old, but only lived there one year. My brother liked Brooklyn because he could go crabbing on the river, but I was afraid of the goats, which chased one of my friends one day. So we came back to New York, and my father bought a house in Ninth Street. . . .

I forgot to say I have a little niece, nearly as old as I am, and she lives in the country. Her mother is my sister, and her father is a clergyman, and I go there in the summer, and she comes here in the winter, and we have things together, like whooping cough and scarlatina. Her name is Ellen and she is very bright. She writes elegant compositions, but I beat her in arithmetic. I hate compositions unless they are on subjects I can look up in books. . . .

New York is getting very big and building up. I walk some mornings with my nurse before breakfast from our house in Ninth Street up Fifth Avenue to Twenty-third Street, and down Broadway home. An officer stands in front of the House of Refuge on Madison Square, ready to arrest bad people, and he looks as if he would like to find some.

Fifth Avenue is very muddy above Eighteenth Street, and there are no blocks of houses as there are downtown, but only two or three on a block. Last Saturday we had a picnic on the grounds of Mr. Waddell's country seat way up Fifth Avenue, and it was so muddy I spoiled my new light cloth gaiter boots. I have a beautiful green and black changeable silk visite, but my mother said it looked like rain and I could not wear it, and it never rained a drop after all. It has a pinked ruffle all around it and a sash behind.

Parlor games took place in the evenings in wealthier homes in the East, but many settler children in the West played the same games on winter nights when there was less work to do. Most American families in the 1800s observed the Sabbath, which meant that no work was allowed on Sundays. Children were expected to read and play quiet games on Sundays. Outdoor games were played whenever kids had a chance—when their chores were done and during recess at school.

During the nineteenth century, America was changing. Many of the experiences we now associate with American childhood first became common during that time. Americans had ideas about how they wanted the country to develop and many of those ideas related directly to the development of American youth. Educating children took on new importance, and schools were built across the country, forever changing the lives of children.

If their families were wealthy, nineteenth-century children would enjoy childhoods not so different from later generations of children, where most of their lives were spent in play and studies. Even in poorer homes, though, the Sabbath—Sunday— was a day for quiet enjoyments like looking at books or playing quiet games.

Part II
School

During the early nineteenth century, America was still establishing itself, settling new land, building communities that would turn into cities, defining it's identity in the world. That took a lot of work, and not just on a political level. Individual people had to support their families, build their homes, defend themselves against the threats of weather and disease, as well as help run local governments. Hardships were many, and as a result, everyone needed to lend a hand. Children couldn't opt out of jobs because they were busy playing, or they had homework to do. There was too much to be done to keep the family alive and the country moving forward. So kids worked, just like everyone else did.

But as the country began to settle down after the Revolutionary War, what it meant to be a young American began to slowly change. Adults' expectations of their children began to change as well—and while plenty of kids were still expected to stay home and work, more and more children began to go to school.

During the first half of the 1800s, most Americans still lived on farms, where there was lots of work for everyone, including the children of the family.

Schools in the nineteenth century were very different than they are today, but one thing was much the same—the blackboard.

You probably take the big blackboard at the front or side of your classroom for granted, but at the beginning of the 1800s, schools had no large blackboards for the entire class to see. Instead, in the few schools that existed in America, children had individual slates at their desks. The teacher would come around from student to student, and write and erase math problems and letters.

Mr. George Baron, an instructor at West Point Military Academy, is con-sidered to be the first American teacher to incorporate the use of a large black chalk board into the presentation of his math lessons in 1801. The benefits of using a single board that everyone in the class could see was immediately obvious to teachers, but not all schools could afford the slate needed for making a blackboard. Still, blackboards saved teachers re-writing and allowed them to educate larger numbers of students easily. Before long, blackboards were seen as a necessity in the classroom rather than a luxury. Slabs of slate were ordered and shipped across America on the ever-expanding railroad systems, and even single-room schoolhouses in the most rural areas of the country began enjoying the use of this innovative teaching tool. By the mid-1800s, blackboards could be found in almost every school. They had become the single most important educational tool, and they remained the primary all-around educational fixture in schoolrooms and businesses for almost two hundred years. For better or worse, this breakthrough in teaching, changed the way teachers taught. No longer did teachers teach individuals; now they taught groups. Blackboards had placed teachers at the head of the class.

Before blackboards were invented, each child had an individual slate like this that she wrote on at her desk. The teacher would then come around and look at her work—or write more work for her to do on the slate.

As simple as this late nineteenth-century classroom is, it has a blackboard at the front of the room.

Other changes were going on in the classrooms of the 1800s as well. Nowadays, most kids attend school for nine or ten months—but in the nineteenth century, if a child attended school at all, it was for only a few months (or in some

Girls in Eastern cities sometimes attended girls' schools where women teachers taught them subjects such as reading, languages, art, and household skills.

cases, weeks) per year. The reason for such limited time in school was that children were expected to contribute to the work of the family. Only the richest families in the Northeast and South could afford to have their children educated year round.

Sometimes young scholars fresh out of college might fill in a year or two as a

In the eighteenth and early nineteenth centuries, wealthy families often hired a tutor to educate their sons.

EYEWITNESS ACCOUNT

Selections from Didy's Diary

Monday 25th, October 1841

I got up early as this was the day I was to go to school and stayed in the parlor writing until breakfast was ready. After breakfast Aunt Henrietta Matilda put up my hair and then Aunt Eleanora and Aunt Maria went up to Madam Bujac's [the school] with me. Tom the servant went too carrying a basket with my books. We went in and Madame Bujac took me into the school room and Miss Thayer asked me what books I had learnt in. I showed her and she gave me some grammar to learn. . . . Then I went back to the schoolroom and a little while afterward I went with the other girls up stairs to take lessons in drawing and when this was done, school was out but I went down into the schoolroom and went on learning my lesson as I did not know any of the girls. . . . I went into the dining room to Madam Bujac who heard me my phrases and made me read French and translate. Then I went back to the schoolroom and soon afterwards school was out. I began to run in the garden after Blance Bujac and Agnes Riddle and while we were running about Tom came and told me that the carriage was waiting for me.

private tutor for the children of a white plantation owner in the South or a rich Northern businessman before settling on a profession. The tutors would have been treated as one of the family, living in the home (think what it would be like having your teacher live with you!), and teaching all the children in the family who were old enough to learn. And in some cases, wealthy children were sent to private academies to prepare them for college.

But less wealthy families also made sure their children were educated. In the nineteenth century, most white American children between the ages of five and fifteen received at least some schooling—and sometimes children as young as two or three were sent off to school with their older brothers or sisters! Education was not confined to a classroom. Many sons and daughters learned the basics of reading, writing, and mathematics from their parents, enough that they could read the Bible or settle an account. There were remote back-country families where children received no education whatsoever, and entire communities could neither read nor write, but as whole, white America was surprisingly literate.

School buildings were built across America, mostly simple, one-room structures, often poorly built with no windows, sometimes miles from children's houses. (Kids had to walk to school, as there were no school busses!) The single classroom was often overcrowded, especially during the times of the year when children could be most easily spared from farm work. Imagine going to school

The typical school for most children in the 1800s was a small, one-room building like this.

The interior of the school building would have looked much like this. Heat was provided by a wood stove, so those students whose desks were at the back of the room might feel quite chilly on winter days.

with as many as eighty different kids in the same room, all different ages, from very young children to teenagers!

School days would be considered short by today's standards, sometimes only going from 8 or 9 a.m. to 1 p.m., to accommodate children's duties at home. Those four or five hours, however, could be amazingly boring! They would be filled with memorization through repetition—a classroom full of children doing the same math problems over and over, and reciting together unison the same sentences. "Rote" learning was the style, and teachers were generally not well trained in any more creative methods of instruction. Many teachers, in fact, especially in the Western states, were teenage girls, barely older than their students.

INCREDIBLE INDIVIDUAL
Horace Mann

One of the biggest advocates for publicly available education was Horace Mann. As a member of the Massachusetts senate, he lobbied for the development of a state board of education, and in 1837, when the state board of education was established, he became the secretary. From this position, Mann was able to introduce many reforms. He established what were known as "normal schools"—schools specifically designed to train teachers, so that competently trained professionals were teaching children. During the 1840s, he also helped to establish "common schools"—what we think of today as public elementary schools. He visited the schools of other countries to get ideas of how to improve his system and instituted a program of annual reports to be sure the schools in his state were being held to a standard. It was largely due to his twelve years in charge of Massachusetts' education that the state became the model on which other school systems in the country were based.

In the "more civilized" East, however, schools were better established. In 1821, the first American public high school, English High School, opened in Boston. It focused on teaching young, working class boys what they would need for business and engineering trades. This stood in contrast to other schools, like some of the private academies, that focused more on scholarly

The Boston English High School provided free education to boys (but not girls).

pursuits and prepared schoolboys for college. Best of all, English High School was free. That meant publicly funded education had begun.

In 1852, Massachusetts passed the first mandatory attendance law. Although it was rarely enforced and did not require a lengthy commitment on the part of each individual student, it spoke volumes about the importance Massachusetts placed on the education of its youth. By 1885, sixteen other states had followed suit.

"Normal schools" offered all children educational opportunities. These turn-of-the-century children are practicing brushing their teeth at a normal school in Washington, DC.

Black families on the frontier were often excluded from attending school.

For black children, however, the story was completely different. In the South, before the Civil War, formal education was almost completely unavailable for the children of slaves. Slaves were kept illiterate on purpose, and in many Southern states it was the law. A slave who was caught reading—or trying to learn in any capacity—risked being punished. In the second half of the nineteenth century, however, that began to change, and education became more available to all children.

During the years of the Civil War, the focus of the entire nation had shifted to other topics, and the forward momentum Mann had developed was slowed. Children were pulled from school to help tend to farms and look after young children as fathers went off to war. Drummer boys, often only eleven years old or younger, marched into war with military units. Young ladies helped their mothers raise funds and collect supplies for soldiers.

But the cause of education did not fall forgotten entirely, and in 1867, just

During the Civil War, young boys went into active combat as drummer boys—and were often wounded or even killed.

two years after the end of the war, the Federal Department of Education was founded to help assess what individual states needed to establish effective school systems.

In the years following the Civil War, Congress required states to provide education to children, but Southern children were often needed at home to help during the Reconstruction and did not attend. Many white Southerners also opposed educating black children, but by the mid–1870s, hundreds of thousands of black children were attending school. Schools were segregated, however, keeping black children separated from white children in schools that were usually of lesser quality.

INCREDIBLE INDIVIDUAL
Homer Plessy

You have probably heard of Rosa Parks, who wouldn't give up her bus seat and helped start the Montgomery Bus Boycott in 1955. But have you heard of Homer Plessy? He also refused to move from a seat, but the result of his action was very different.

In 1892, Homer Plessy sat in a car on the Louisiana Railroad that was supposed to be for white people only. Plessy, being one-eighth black and seven-eights white, was technically considered black under Louisiana law, so he was asked to move to the "colored" car. When he refused, he was arrested and sent to jail.

Plessy argued against the treatment in the case, Homer Adolph Plessy v. The State of Louisiana. The judge, John Howard Ferguson, ruled against Plessy. The case went on to the Supreme Court of Louisiana, where the ruling was upheld.

The case created the legal basis for the "separate but equal" viewpoint that made segregation acceptable in most of America until the Supreme Court ruled against it in Brown v. Board of Education in 1954.

SNAPSHOT FROM THE PAST

Finally!

I remember the first day the
Freedman's School was open. It was
odd and wonderful. I didn't know
what to expect. And I was afraid I
would stick out because of how little

I knew. But there were so many of us, crammed into that little room, of so many
different ages, that as soon as I sat down I felt as though I'd be fine. One woman
must have been eighty if she was a day! It was incredible to see free black men and
women able to take advantage of this. And everyone made such an effort to look the
part of scholars. As some of us walked to school (how exciting it is to say that!), we
were passed by some young whites who gave us looks of judgment but said nothing.
And I have a feeling it is because we were dressed unexpectedly. They still must
think of us as animals. But we are not. And soon we will be able to read and write
as well as them.

Miss Nelson, the young white woman who came from the North to teach at the
school, was very well organized. We spent five hours learning different things—
beginning with reading and moving on to mathematics. For some of us it was harder
than for others, and with the class being so large, I think it put an awful strain on
Miss Nelson. I myself had the most trouble with my math. But we made it through
that first day.

The school building was not much more than a barn. And the materials we had
to use for our lessons were scarce. But we were excited nonetheless to return the
next day. And, although she didn't show much emotion, Miss Nelson made a point
of telling us that she saw potential in each and every one of us, and that she hoped
all of us would be returning to continue our studies. She also warned us that the
lessons would get more challenging, but after so many years of wanting to know how
to read and write, I knew I was ready.

Toward the end of the century, the educational reform that began with colleges and high schools made its way down through the grades to the youngest Americans. Kindergarten programs spread westward out of New England, popping up in cities as far west as St. Louis and Chicago.

In the West, the quality and availability of schools depended on where you lived. The families of frontier children often lived long distances from any town, and the kids were still likely to be spending most of their time helping on the farm. Children were taught at home until, as their communities grew, schools were built and teachers were hired.

American Indian children were also provided with free schooling, although the Christian missionaries, hoping to convert them, were often their teachers. Boarding schools for Native children removed kids from their families—and tried to remove their culture from them at the same time. America's goal in educating these children, unfortunately, was to "kill the Indian and save the man."

Children might have to walk long distances to attend a school like this. As a result, attendance would vary, depending on the time of the year and what work needed doing at home.

EYEWITNESS ACCOUNT

Lone Wolf of the Blackfoot Tribe remembered what it was like to go to a boarding school:

[Long hair] was the pride of all Indians. The boys, one by one, would break down and cry when they saw their braids thrown on the floor. All of the buckskin clothes had to go and we had to put on the clothes of the White Man. If we thought the days were bad, the nights were much worse. This is when the loneliness set in, for it was when we knew that we were all alone. Many boys ran away from the school because the treatment was so bad, but most of them were caught and brought back by the police.

Indian children were often taken from their families and sent to live at boarding schools, where they were taught how to be "white."

More children, spending more time in school with better teachers, meant there was now a much larger audience to be reached with popular books. Authors began writing for these newly literate youngsters, and the late nineteenth century brought some of the most beloved and widely read books of all time, many of which are classics, still being read by America's youth today—books like Louisa May Alcott's *Little Women* in 1868, or Mark Twain's *Tom Sawyer* in 1876.

But not all children in the nineteenth century were attending school. Other children were not so lucky. In the tenements of big cities like New York, children lived far different lives.

Recess was an important time in a child's life, a rare opportunity to play with other kids.

Part III
Work

If you had been a kid during the early 1800s, no matter where in the country you lived, there was a good chance you would have lived on a farm—or at the very least, your family depended on the land to some extent. And because your family depended so heavily on that land, they could not afford to neglect it. Everyone had to help, including the kids.

And if you didn't happen to live in a rural area, odds were good (unless your family was wealthy) you'd still be expected to contribute to your family's income.

The Industrial Revolution was in full swing by the end of the 1800s in America—and children were some of the workers who helped run the new factories being built.

Calling it a "revolution" makes it sound like it happened overnight, but that isn't quite true. Throughout the 1800s, more machines were being introduced into the workplace.

Even very young children worked in the fields. This little girl helped her parents pick strawberries in California from the time she was five years old.

Factories changed the look of
America—and they changed the
lives of many Americans as well.

At the same time, railroads were expanding like a web to the far corners of the United States. Slowly but surely, America changed from a rural to an urban society. More people moved to the cities looking for jobs, usually leaving a farming life behind. They weren't alone, either. Huge immigrant populations from Ireland, Poland, Germany, and Italy arrived in the new cities in waves. They too were looking for city jobs.

The U.S. population was swelling, creating a demand for more products, and the population of cities was growing at the same pace. From the year 1800 to the year 1890, the U.S. population grew from about 5 million people

During the nineteenth century, immigrants to the United States brought with them hopes and dreams for a better life. The "New World" was not always kind to them, however.

Trains brought other changes to America, allowing them to be connected in new ways.

to 63 million people, more than twelve times its original size! And most of these new citizens lived in cities, where they worked at jobs that were far removed from the farming work so common at the end of the eighteenth century.

The "revolution" was not kind to everyone. New conditions in cities meant new opportunities, but not all of them were good. As industry boomed and new jobs arrived, so did the workplace dangers and negligence of bad employers. Unions formed to protect people from abuse, and reformers entered the cities, arguing for better living conditions for the extremely poor immigrants. While it may have allowed the United States to grow into a powerful nation, it did so at the expense of its poorest classes of people.

Some children of the poorest families were even "given" to factory owners permanently. Factories used children to run machines because they were cheaper labor than adults. Child labor became a major issue during the nineteenth century; as early as 1810, close to two million children were working fifty to seventy hours a week in factories. These children were often younger than seven, and the conditions where they worked were unhealthy

Children in factories worked harder than most adults do today. The jobs were dangerous, and the buildings were unhealthy.

These boys are working at a cotton mill.

and dangerous. They certainly were not granted time for an education.

Children were put to work in all kinds of places. In textile mills, where cloth was made, they started working as young as five years old. Their small size made them perfect for dangerous tasks like climbing atop a spinning frame to mend broken threads or put back empty bobbins. They worked from 7 a.m. to 5:30 p.m. and sometimes much longer, usually for less than 50 cents a day. The children who worked in the mines started working when they were five years old, pulling cartloads of coal through tight passages. Their lives were so unhealthy and dangerous that most weren't expected to live past twenty-five.

Children did odd jobs of all kinds: they carried boxes of hats for a retail store, or in coastal cities they shucked oysters and picked shrimp for a few dollars a month. Some children were bootblacks in the cities, carrying a rag and a tin of polish, stopping wealthy men to shine their shoes. Others were "bowling alley boys" who worked well past midnight, setting up pins for the bowlers. Sometimes they were orphans, brought from faraway to work in cities for a boss who'd adopted them into a kind of forced labor. Sometimes they simply needed to make a few extra cents for their poor families.

Being a chimney sweep was one of the worst jobs given to young children in the 1800s. Because they were small enough to fit inside chimneys, they were given the task of cleaning out the soot. The job was dangerous, and breathing the soot and smoke was bad for the children's lungs.

SNAPSHOT FROM THE PAST
The Life of a Factory Child

Jimmy Barns was born in the year 1875—and five years later, he went to work in a metal factory. By the time he was twelve, he was as exhausted as an old man. He never had time to play; he seldom had enough to eat. But he had nine younger brothers and sisters, and his family depended on his income, small as it was.

On a hot summer day, Jimmy struggled to stay awake while doing the monotonous work that was his job. He had gotten up at four-thirty, begun work at five-thirty, and now, his head nodded—but he jerked awake when the overseer gave him a sharp rap on the head.

"You were nearly ten minutes late this morning," the overseer growled, "and now you're falling asleep on the job. I'm going to have to dock you a week's pay. We'll see if that teaches you to do the job you're being paid to do."

Tears sprang into Jimmy's eyes, but he blinked them away and went back to work.

At ten o'clock, the workers took a fifteen-minute break to eat their breakfast. Jimmy slurped down the thin soup and wolfed the dry piece of bread. Then he went back to work. He was dreading going home tonight and telling his mother that his pay would be docked. She would cry, he knew, because they were counting on his paycheck to buy groceries—and now the little ones would go hungry.

But by six o'clock that evening, Jimmy was too tired to think about anything except getting home. He trudged back to the crowded tenement where he lived with his family, eager to eat some supper and fall into bed.

Tomorrow, he would do it all again.

Although generally there was a movement developing in the country to be sure children were being educated, not all were so lucky. Immigrant children especially struggled to get instruction, having to rely on the few "public" schoolhouses available at the time.

Today, you might feel as though school expects a lot out of you—but

By the end of the 1800s, many people were upset that the United States' economy depended so heavily on children's labor.

The late nineteenth century brought with it a movement to make sure that all children were in school, not in factories.

most children during the nineteenth century would probably think your life was incredibly luxurious, compared to the responsibilities they were expected to shoulder. Even outside the factories, children were still expected to work long days (even if they went to school as well). On farms in the North, South, East, and West, children were waking before dawn to begin their day. The boys, if they were strong enough (usually by about age eight), helped their fathers in the fields. They would ride and steady the plow horses, plant seeds, weed the fields, and bind the wheat. And in the winter they'd help split wood, build fences, and haul firewood.

SNAPSHOT FROM THE PAST
A Man's Work

Although he had only turned twelve a few weeks earlier, Daniel knew the exact day he considered himself a man. It happened at harvest time, on the second day his father had let him wield the sickle. The previous morning his father had woken him earlier than usual and they had eaten breakfast in silence. But once they were outside, his father explained the early start to the morning. "Daniel, I want you to hold this and take some practice swings. You're old enough and strong enough to work with me in the field now. And I could sure use your help." Daniel ran to his father's side and reached for the sickle. But his father stopped him. "Daniel! This is no toy. The blade is sharper than it looks. And it's heavy. Treat it with respect or it'll disrespect you." Daniel nodded.

At the end of that day he came in from the fields exhausted, his hands calloused. But he felt like he had accomplished little. The second day though, Daniel was swinging away at the wheat, guiding the sickle with his right hand, and collecting the stalks in his left, just as his father had shown him. But with one mighty swing, the blade slipped and tore the flesh of his left hand.

He screamed, and his father dropped his sickle and ran to him. Daniel's hand was covered in blood, but it wasn't as bad as Daniel had thought at first. His father laughed and said, "No boy becomes a good reaper until he cuts his left hand."

As Daniel walked toward the well to rinse off the blood, he looked back and caught his father watching him. Daniel squared his shoulders. He felt like a man.

By age sixteen, a boy was doing a full man's work on the farm, with very little time for himself. The idea of individual free time was an idea neither children nor adults considered. Girls were just as busy as boys, although theirs tasks were different. By as young as ten, girls were given the duties of the house; young girls helped to care for the even younger children of the house, as well as the elderly members of the family. Up by 5 a.m. at the latest, a girl might start her day by helping her mother boil potatoes and fry up some pork for breakfast. Then it was time to get the

Little girls were usually expected to help with the family's mending. In a world where new clothes were expensive and hard to come by, repairing ripped clothing and hole-filled socks was an important task.

When your family depended on wood to heat its home, chopping wood was an endless task.

young ones ready for school (if it was that time of year and they were lucky enough to be able to attend) and to tend to the older members of the family. After that, a girl might make preparations for the evening meal. And then it was on to other tasks like mending clothes, milking cows, and cleaning. All of this done alongside her mother, preparing her for the day she would run her own household and have daughters of her own to direct.

INCREDIBLE INDIVIDUAL
Charles Loring Brace

Charles Loring Brace saw the lives of orphans and street children in New York City and wanted to make a difference. In 1853 he established the Children's Aid Society, which helped provide educational opportunities and care for these needy children. Many of the orphaned children were sent west to live with and work for pioneer families. This movement became known as "The Orphan Train." The children were selected by families to whom they then became indentured—they had no birth certificates, were not adopted, and could not inherit property. Upon turning eighteen, the children were freed and given a small cash payment to start them on their adult lives.

Little children growing up in the late 1800s for the first time faced the likelihood of childhoods that would revolve around play and education, rather than work.

Think About It

The average American childhood has changed very much since the 1800s. In many 19th-century families, children needed to make an economic contribution, either working on the farm or outside the home, at as early an age as possible, and children's lives revolved around work. Today, childhood is a time when education and recreation are considered much more important than they were in the past.

- How do you think an average American young person, about your age, thought of themselves in the 1800s?

- How do you think going to work instead of going to school affected the later lives of children in the 1800s?

- What are some of the basic things about being a kid that have changed since the 1800s?

- Are there things that you think might not have changed about being a young person?

Words Used in This Book

boarding schools: Institutions where students both live and go to school. Wealthy children were often sent away from home for their education; Native American children were sometimes forced to go to government-run boarding schools.

empowered: Having a sense of being in control of your own life.

intricate: Something with a complicated design.

mandatory: Required by rule or law, without exception.

negligence: Carelessness and lack of concern for the safety of others.

nimbleness: Speed, lightness, and accuracy in movement.

reformers: People who work for the improvement of social problems, such as dangerous working conditions for children.

scarlatina: A mild form of scarlet fever, a contagious disease that often affected young people in large numbers during outbreaks in the 1800s. Symptoms include a red rash covering most of the body and a high fever.

whooping cough: A highly contagious disease common in children in the 1800s. Symptoms include a violent cough and a "whooping" sound when breathing in.

Find Out More

In Books

Holt, Marilyn. *Children of the Western Plains: The Nineteenth Century Experience.* Chicago, Ill.: Ivan R. Dee, 2003.

King, Wilma. *Stolen Childhood: Slave Youth in Nineteenth-Century America.* Bloomington, Ind.: Indiana University Press, 1997.

Marten, James. *Children and Youth in a New Nation.* New York: New York University Press, 1999.

On the Internet

Child Labor in America
memory.loc.gov/learn/lessons/98/labor/resource.html

One-room Schoolhouse Resource Center
littleredschoolhousehistoricalsociety.schools.officelive.com/resourcecenter.aspx

Victorian Toys and Hobbies
www.victorianbazaar.com/hobbies.html

The websites listed in this book were active at the time of publication. The publisher is not responsible for websites that have changed their address or discontinued operation since the date of publication. The publisher will review and update the websites upon each reprint.

Index

About the Author and the Consultant

Matthew Ronald Strange is a writer living in Richmond, Virginia. He has worked as an editor and as a copywriter, but his true passion is writing creatively: short stories, poetry, and maybe someday a novel. This is his first time writing for Mason Crest.

John Gillis is a Rutgers University Professor of History Emeritus. A graduate of Amherst College and Stanford University, he has taught at Stanford, Princeton, University of California at Berkeley, as well as Rutgers. Gillis is well known for his work in social history, including pioneering studies of age relations, marriage, and family. The author or editor of ten books, he has also been a fellow at both St. Antony's College, Oxford, and Clare Hall, Cambridge.

Picture Credits

Creative Commons: pp. 12–13, 14, 16–17, 18–19, 20–21, 22, 24–25, 26, 32, 37, 45, 59
Dover: p. 33
Grobe, Hannes; Creative Commons: p. 30
Library of Congress: pp. 23, 27, 31, 34, 35, 42, 43, 44, 46, 47, 54–55, 57, 58
Minnesota Historical Society: p. 56

To the best knowledge of the publisher, all images not specifically credited are in the public domain. If any image has been inadvertently uncredited, please notify Harding House Publishing Service, 220 Front Street, Vestal, New York 13850, so that credit can be given in future printings.